DEFENDING OUR NATION

PUTTING OUT FIRES:
FIREFIGHTERS

DEFENDING OUR NATION

PUTTING OUT FIRES:
FIREFIGHTERS

FOREWORD BY
MANNY GOMEZ, ESQ., SECURITY AND TERRORISM EXPERT

BY
BRENDA RALPH LEWIS

MASON CREST

Mason Crest
450 Parkway Drive, Suite D
Broomall, PA 19008
www.masoncrest.com

Printed in the United States of America
First printing
9 8 7 6 5 4 3 2 1

Series ISBN: 978-1-4222-3759-5
Hardcover ISBN: 978-1-4222-3769-4
ebook ISBN: 978-1-4222-8025-6

Library of Congress Cataloging-in-Publication Data

Names: Lewis, Brenda Ralph, author.
Title: Putting out fires : firefighters / foreword by Manny Gomez, Esq.,
  Security and Terrorism Expert ; by Brenda Ralph Lewis.
Other titles: Firefighters
Description: Broomall, Pennsylvania : Mason Crest, [2018] | Series: Defending
  our nation | Includes bibliographical references and index.
Identifiers: LCCN 2016053108| ISBN 9781422237694 (hardback) | ISBN
  9781422237595 (series) | ISBN 9781422280256 (ebook)
Subjects: LCSH: Fire fighters--Juvenile literature. | Fire   extinction--Juvenile
  literature. | Wildfires--Juvenile literature. | Fires--History--Juvenile literature.
Classification: LCC HD8039.F5 L49 2018 | DDC 628.9/25--dc23

Developed and Produced by Print Matters Productions, Inc. (www.printmattersinc.com)
Cover and Interior Design by Bill Madrid, Madrid Design
Additional Text by Kelly Kagamas Tomkies

CONTENTS

KEY ICONS TO LOOK FOR:

 Words to understand: These words with their easy-to-understand definitions will increase the reader's understanding of the text while building vocabulary skills.

 Sidebars: This boxed material within the main text allows readers to build knowledge, gain insights, explore possibilities, and broaden their perspectives by weaving together additional information to provide realistic and holistic perspectives.

 Educational Videos: Readers can view videos by scanning our QR codes, providing them with additional educational content to supplement the text. Examples include news coverage, moments in history, speeches, iconic sports moments and much more!

 Text-dependent questions: These questions send the reader back to the text for more careful attention to the evidence presented there.

 Research projects: Readers are pointed toward areas of further inquiry connected to each chapter. Suggestions are provided for projects that encourage deeper research and analysis.

 Series glossary of key terms: This back-of-the book glossary contains terminology used throughout this series. Words found here increase the reader's ability to read and comprehend higher-level books and articles in this field.

FOREWORD

VIGILANCE

We live in a world where we have to have a constant state of awareness—about our surroundings and who is around us. Law enforcement and the intelligence community cannot predict or stop the next terrorist attack alone. They need the citizenry of America, of the world, to act as a force multiplier in order to help deter, detect, and ultimately defeat a terrorist attack.

Technology is ever evolving and is a great weapon in the fight against terrorism. We have facial recognition, we have technology that is able to detect electronic communications through algorithms that may be related to terrorist activity—we also have drones that could spy on communities and bomb them without them ever knowing that a drone was there and with no cost of life to us.

But ultimately it's human intelligence and inside information that will help defeat a potential attack. It's people being aware of what's going on around them: if a family member, neighbor, coworker has suddenly changed in a manner where he or she is suddenly spouting violent anti-Western rhetoric or radical Islamic fundamentalism, those who notice it have a duty to report it to authorities so that they can do a proper investigation.

In turn, the trend since 9/11 has been for international communication as well as federal and local communication. Gone are the days when law enforcement or intelligence organizations kept information to themselves and didn't dare share it for fear that it might compromise the integrity of the information or for fear that the other organization would get equal credit. So the NYPD wouldn't tell anything to the FBI, the FBI wouldn't tell the CIA, and the CIA wouldn't tell the British counterintelligence agency, MI6, as an example. Improved as things are, we could do better.

We also have to improve global propaganda. Instead of dropping bombs, drop education on individuals who are even considering joining ISIS. Education is salvation. We have the greatest production means in the world through Hollywood and so on, so why don't we match ISIS materials? We tried it once but the government itself tried to produce it. This is something that should definitely be privatized. We also need to match the energy of cyber attackers—and we need savvy youth for that.

There are numerous ways that you could help in the fight against terror—joining law enforcement, the military, or not-for-profit organizations like the Peace Corps. If making the world a safer place appeals to you, draw on your particular strengths and put them to use where they are needed. But everybody should serve and be part of this global fight against terrorism in some small way. Certainly, everybody should be a part of the fight by simply being aware of their surroundings and knowing when something is not right and acting on that sense. In the investigation after most successful attacks, we know that somebody or some persons or people knew that there was something wrong with the person or persons who perpetrated the attack. Although it feels awkward to tell the authorities that you believe somebody is acting suspicious and may be a terrorist sympathizer or even a terrorist, we have a higher duty not only to society as a whole but to our family, friends, and ultimately ourselves to do something to ultimately stop the next attack.

It's not *if* there is going to be another attack, but where, when, and how. So being vigilant and being proactive are the orders of the day.

Manny Gomez, Esq.
President of MG Security Services,
Chairman of the National Law Enforcement Association,
former FBI Special Agent, U.S. Marine, and NYPD Sergeant

CHAPTER 1

FIREFIGHTING IN THE PAST

The Great Fire of London in 1666.

F ire has always been important in everyday life. It provides warmth and security, but it can also be dangerous and destructive. In prehistoric times, it was used to warm caves and cook food; big fires were lit at night at the entrance to the caves so that wild animals would be frightened away. However, fires can also burn out of control, burning down entire forests, or turning houses and other buildings into smoking ashes. Fire can kill people by burning them to death or by choking them with the smoke it creates.

Recording of 9/11 firefighters' last moments.

Fires in the Cities

The danger of fire became even greater some 6,000 years ago when people began to live in cities in and around Mesopotamia, present-day Iraq. The ancient Egyptians were well aware of this and used hand-operated wooden pumps to put out fires in the second century BCE. The problem in the ancient cities was that people lived close together: they had their own fires and cooking stoves, so a single outbreak of fire could quickly spread, destroying homes and killing people. In the towns and cities of the ancient Roman Empire, this happened all too often in badly built, overcrowded three- or four-story apartment blocks called **insulae**, or islands.

Words to Understand

Insulae: Roman apartment blocks.

Conflagration: Large destructive fire.

Firebreaks: Area of land that has had plants and trees removed to stop the spread of fire.

All it took to start a fire and, often burn down the entire building, was for someone to have an accident while cooking a meal. Starting in one apartment, the blaze could spread through the insula within a few minutes and then threaten neighboring buildings. This was why there were teams of vigiles, or watchmen, who patrolled the streets of Roman cities. Their primary job was to deal with any sort of trouble—including fights or murders—but they were also the firefighters who dealt with blazing buildings, putting out the fires and rescuing people trapped by the flames. There were 7,000 vigiles in ancient Rome itself.

Unfortunately, the vigiles were not always successful. Certainly, they were unable to handle a really big fire, like the huge **conflagration** that destroyed two-thirds of ancient Rome in CE 64. It started on July 18 in the Circus Maximus, a place of public entertainment where chariot races were held, and it burned for more than a week. Ten of Rome's 14 districts were completely destroyed, as temples, public buildings, and thousands of homes went up in flames. There were terrible scenes as Romans ran out of the city, screaming in panic.

A Fireman's Prayer

When I am called to duty, God
Wherever flames may rage
Give me the strength to save some life
Whatever be its age
Help me embrace a little child
Before it is too late
Or save an older person from
The horror of that fate
Enable me to be alert and
Hear the weakest shout
And quickly and efficiently
To put the fire out . . .
And if according to Your will
I have to lose my life
Please bless with Your protecting hand
My children and my wife
(Anonymous)

Nero, the Roman Emperor, was not in Rome when the fire started, but 33 miles (53 km) away to the south, at Antium, modern Anzio. He seems to have done his best to help, organizing food supplies and setting up temporary homes. All the same, a rumor spread that he was the one who had set Rome alight. It was said he wanted to build himself a larger palace and thought that Rome was so run-down it deserved to be destroyed. According to the gossips, Nero stood on the roof of his palace and "fiddled," or played, his lyre while Rome burned. No one knows if any of this was true, but after the fire, Nero set about rebuilding Rome as a much more splendid city, with fine buildings and a grid system of roads.

This painting by Henryk Siemiradzki depicts the burning of Rome, supposedly set by Nero.

London's Burning

Three years earlier, another city of the Roman empire—London, capital of the Roman province of Britannia—went up in flames when a rebel British queen, Boudicca, attacked the city and burned it. After this, in CE 63, the Romans decided to appoint vigiles to look out for fires in London. London kept its vigiles until the Romans abandoned Britannia in around CE 426, returning to Rome to defend it against attacks by barbarian tribes. Unfortunately, the vigiles departed with the Romans, and London had no proper fire service for another 1,250 years.

In 1212, London Bridge burned down. The consequences were severe. Not only were 12,000 people reported to have died, but London Bridge was at that time the only bridge across the Thames River, which runs through the city.

The burning of London Bridge was known as the Great Fire of London until an even greater and much more damaging fire broke out in September 1666. At that time, London still had no fire service—the capital's first fire brigade was not formed until 1680. This great fire burned for over four days, and the flames burned down most of London's big buildings, including Saint Paul's Cathedral, and destroyed around 13,000 homes. The flames could be seen nearly

This painting depicts what the Great Fire of London would have looked like at a distance.

40 miles (64 km) away. The fire began in a baker's shop in Pudding Lane and spread rapidly. Before long, a huge cloud of black, choking smoke, "like the top of a burning oven," hung over the city. The king of England, Charles II, and his brother James, Duke of York, helped to fight the flames by organizing firefighting teams and pulling down buildings to make **firebreaks**. But the flames leapt across the firebreaks, and John Evelyn, a famous English diarist, described what followed:

> There was nothing heard or seen but crying out and lamentation, running about like distracted creatures as [the fire] burned both in breadth and length, leaping from house to house and street to street; for the heat had even ignited the air, and the fire devoured houses, furniture, and everything.

It took a long time for London to recover from this disaster. Many Londoners were unable to return to the city to live until 1672, six years later.

Benjamin Franklin and his son flying a kite during an electrical storm.

Benjamin Franklin and the Lightning Rod

In colonial America, Boston got its first fire brigade in the same year as London—1680. The firefighters were paid to put out fires, but in 1735, Benjamin Franklin had a different idea. He formed the first volunteer fire department in Philadelphia, believing that putting out fires should be a public duty.

Franklin was also worried by the thatched straw roofs most Americans put on their houses. It was far too easy for sparks or embers from chimneys to set the roofs on fire. Another problem was lightning strikes that hit the roofs during thunderstorms and set them ablaze. To stop this from happening, Benjamin Franklin invented the lightning rod. This makes the lightning discharge into the ground and prevents it from setting houses on fire.

The Bucket Brigades

At first, there were no fire engines that could pump out water to extinguish the flames. Instead, there were bucket brigades—long lines of people who passed buckets of water to each other until they reached the fire, where the water was thrown onto the blaze. Obviously, this was not very effective, because there was usually too little water to stop the fire from spreading.

When fire engines, pulled by horses, were introduced in the late 18th century, the bucket brigades were used to fill up their reservoirs, or stores, of water. This was dangerous. The pumps used were not very powerful, which meant bringing the engines too close to the fire, or at least as close as the terrified horses would allow. It was not until the 19th century that more powerful, steam-driven pumps and better water hoses began to be used.

Did You Know?
- George Washington brought the first fire engine to America from England in 1765.
- Long before he became president, George Washington was a volunteer firefighter with the fire company in Alexandria, VA.
- Dalmatian dogs were used to guard engines and equipment when fire companies used to compete with each other to attend fires. This was because one way of getting the better of rivals was to steal or damage their equipment.
- The Polish city of Znin was either partly or completely destroyed by fire no less than six times—in 1447, 1494, 1688, 1692, 1700, and 1751.

The Great Chicago Fire of 1871

Despite these advances, however, fire was a still a fearsome destroyer. This was once again demonstrated in Chicago in October 1871, when a fierce blaze started in a barn owned by the O'Leary family in the northern part of the city. The fire quickly went out of control and spread throughout the city. The flames were soon swallowing up houses, buildings, and large mansions.

At this time, many homes were built of wood, and this fed the fire. The flames leapt across the Chicago River and, on the other side, set alight everything in their path. The inhabitants of Chicago fled, cramming the roads out of the city. Not all of them escaped unharmed: some 300 people were killed. Another 100,000, unfortunately, lost their homes.

The view from the west side of the Great Chicago Fire.

The Cow That Started A Fire

It was said that a cow belonging to Mrs. O'Leary started the Great Chicago Fire of 1871, which destroyed the center of the city. A popular song was later written about it:

> Late one night, when we were all in bed,
> Mrs. O'Leary lit a lantern in the shed.
> Her cow kicked it over
> Then winked her eye and said:
> "There'll be a hot time in the old town tonight!"

Firefighting Today

Fortunately, firefighting methods are much more efficient today than they were in 1871. The use of high-tech equipment has greatly improved the firefighters' chances of controlling a blaze. Even so, the battle against fire continues, and there are more fire dangers than ever before. These can be caused by gas explosions in houses or faults in electrical equipment, such as television sets. Chemicals and other inflammable substances can leak from their containers and catch fire. In fact, you could say that firefighting is the longest war in history and that fire is one of the most difficult and dangerous enemies the world has ever faced.

Text-Dependent Questions

1. Who were vigiles in ancient Rome?
2. According to the rumors of the day, why did Nero play his lyre while Rome burned?
3. What famous landmark burned down during the first Great Fire in London in 1212?

Research Projects

1. Why did Benjamin Franklin create the first volunteer fire department? How effective was it?
2. Research how a lightning rod works. How does it prevent lightning strikes and what is its modern-day equivalent?

CHAPTER 2

TRAINING TO BE A FIREFIGHTER

Firefighters in training must participate in rigorous training. Not only do they learn how to successfully diffuse fires, but they learn how to rescue those who are trapped, too, all while wearing heavy uniforms and equipment.

Firefighters must be well trained. The lives of people trapped in a fire depend on them. So do the lives of other members of their firefighting teams.

Everyone is afraid of fire—as they should be, considering the dangers. Firefighters, too, can be afraid, but they still have to do their job. They must do what most people would find terrifying: deliberately go near or into burning buildings and find their way past smoke and flames, collapsing ceilings, and unsafe floors to rescue fire victims. When the firefighters reach these victims, they must be calm and able to reassure them. They must stop victims from panicking so that they can lead them out of danger. Firefighters need great courage to do all this, and they have to show that courage every time they attend a fire.

Even so, it is not enough for firefighters to be brave, healthy, and physically strong. They must also be properly trained, recognizing the dangers they face and knowing how their equipment works and how to use it. There is so much to learn, and firefighters will tell you this—that however long they have been in the fire service, they are always learning more.

What Firefighters Have to Know

The first fact firefighters must learn is that saving lives is their most important task. At the scene of a blaze, firefighters will often use a telephone or radio to discuss the medical problems involved in saving someone's life. In fact, before you can even apply to be a firefighter, you must

Words to Understand

Arson: The crime of deliberately setting a fire.

Breathing apparatus: A helmet and a mask that enable firefighters to breathe when working in the smoke and fumes created by fire.

Spectators: Audience.

Firefighters undergo hours of training not only for fighting fires but also in first aid. They must be sure that victims are stabilized before removing them from a burning building.

be able to show that you have studied emergency first aid, which means that you know how to stop bleeding, how to keep a fire victim's airway clear so that he or she can breathe, and how to move people with broken bones or spines so that they are not injured further.

Firefighters have to be familiar with safety procedures, know how to put on protective clothing and take it off, and know how to handle a **breathing apparatus**. They must learn how to handle big, powerful hoses, how to control a hose when it is pumping water, and how to keep it directed into the fire. Because firefighters use special ropes and knots to pull victims safely out of burning buildings, they also need to know which knots to use and how to tie them.

Then there are the different kinds of fires they will fight: fires in automobiles, buses, and other vehicles; fires in wildlands, where the flames can spread rapidly, especially if the ground is dry and burns easily; fires in places where there are dangerous chemicals or other hazardous materials, which can explode if the flames reach them; and fires in high buildings, where firefighters have to use ladders and platforms to reach the victims.

Many fires are started by acts of carelessness. Throwing a cigarette out the window on a dry day can easily start a fire.

Not all fires start by accident; sometimes **arson** is involved. A fire started deliberately can easily burn out of control. At the end of 2001, bushfires destroyed large areas close to Sydney, Australia, even reaching the edges of the city itself. It was soon discovered that these fires were started by children and young people who had become bored during the school vacation. These irresponsible actions caused tremendous damage.

Arson, of course, is a crime, and arsonists have to be punished for it. So firefighters must always bear in mind that the fire they are fighting could have been deliberately started. Part of their training teaches them to watch out for signs of arson. In a building wrecked by fire, one of these signs might be an empty can of gas, particularly if it is found where a can of gas should not be. Another is the remains of matches or other means of lighting fires. While training, firefighters learn how to recognize these signs and make sure that evidence of them is not disturbed: such information could be important if the arsonist is caught and put on trial.

However, neither can you become a firefighter simply by studying at training courses or taking examinations. On-the-job training is important as well, so trainee firefighters go out with the fire engine teams to the scenes of fires and watch how they handle the emergency. By doing this, trainees can see what the scene of a real fire is like and experience firefighting for themselves.

The Fire Police

Some firefighters are police officers as well, so they have to train and study twice as hard to do their job. The scene of a fire is always dangerous, but the firefighters and their engines and equipment can face extra problems.

Relatives of fire victims can become terrified when they see what is happening to their loved ones, so the fire police have to be there to control them and make sure they do not make the emergency worse.

Quite often, large crowds of spectators gather when a fire breaks out, either to share the excitement of watching the blaze or for some other, less innocent, reason. This is where the fire police come in. They are there to stop people from damaging fire engines or stealing things from them. The crowd may also create difficulties by getting too near to the fire or blocking the road that leads to the scene, which means the fire engines and firefighters cannot get through to the fire. It is the job of the fire police to keep the crowd at a safe distance from a fire. This is often for the spectators' own safety because anything can happen at a fire scene—explosions, debris falling from the burning building, or poisonous fumes or dangerous chemicals escaping from their containers.

Reactions

Some would-be firefighters have romantic ideas about the job. To them, it is exciting and they see themselves as great heroes, valiantly battling the flames and admired by all for doing so. Firefighters are certainly heroes, but their job is not the least bit romantic. Fires are horrifying, and destruction by fire is a fearful sight, for both victims and firefighters. People who cannot face up to these realities are not suited to be firefighters, and this is what some trainees discover when they attend a real fire.

The Size Up

Another important lesson for trainee firefighters to learn is what the fire services call the size up. **Sizing up** is understanding what must be done at the scene of a fire, and every fire is different. For instance, how does the location of a fire affect the way it must be fought? A blaze that starts in open country, with plenty of space around it and probably no other buildings that might also catch fire, is completely different from a fire on a city street, where the buildings are close together.

There are many factors to consider when sizing up a fire. Forest fires can take over a space quite quickly, as can house fires. Forest fires can destroy land, whereas house fires can spread to other homes in the neighborhood.

What is the time of day or night when the fire station receives news of the alarm? If it is a daytime fire, there will be a lot of traffic in the surrounding streets, together with parked automobiles and a large number of people. Obviously, this creates problems. On the other hand, daytime also brings an advantage. Many people are likely to see the fire and raise the alarm, so the fire service can respond quickly. In contrast, if the fire happens at night, the streets will be less busy. This helps, in a way, because there are fewer people in danger and the road to the fire scene is clearer. Yet there is an added problem with a nighttime fire. With fewer people to see it, a night fire in an empty building (for example, a closed department store) might be burning for quite awhile before anyone notices it. As a result, the fire is likely to have done a lot of damage before the firefighters reach it.

Firefighters and Their Families

Firefighters know that they may be killed or injured when they are fighting fires. So when anyone volunteers to become a firefighter, their families become closely involved. Many firefighters are volunteers, because they are located in a rural region or small town that does not have the budget or need to hire a large staff of full-time firefighters. In many small communities most of the firefighters can be volunteers who rotate being on duty and the possibility of getting called in.

"Volunteer Firefighter's Poem"
We are volunteers, we don't get paid for what
   we do
But our hope and prayers are to always see you
   through
We can be eating or awakened in the middle of the
   night
With a blast of our pagers saying, "There is a fire we
   need to fight!"
We are up and dressed and out the door
We meet sirens blaring and trucks that roar
The adrenaline pumping, we're ready to go
Will we make it home? We never know.
Our jobs are to fight fires and to also save a life
Our goal is to make it home to our children and our wife
We do the unexpected. We tread where people fear.
                     (Anonymous)

Another poem is titled, *"I Am a Fireman's Wife"*
The table's set, the meal's prepared,
Our guest will soon arrive.
My husband once more disappears,
with the hope of keeping a child alive.
While waiting at home alone, our plans have gone awry.
My first response is to sit right down and cry.
But soon again I realize the importance of my life
When I agreed to take on the duties of being a
Fireman's Wife.
While there may be drawbacks, I'll take them in my stride.
Knowing "My Daddy saved a life,"
our children can say with pride.
The gusting winds and raging flames may be his final fate.
But with God's help, I can remain my fireman's faithful
   mate.
                     (Anonymous)

What is the weather like? What is the state of the water supply for fighting the fire? How tall is the burning building and on which floor did the fire start? How far has it spread? Is it safe to use fire-axes to break down doors or walls, or has the fire so weakened these structures that there could be a dangerous collapse?

Firefighter puts on full gear in 60 seconds.

These are just some of the many questions firefighters must ask themselves when sizing up. Once finished, they must be confident they know what to do. They cannot afford to think twice or make a mistake; someone might die if they do.

Text-Dependent Questions

1. What is a firefighter's most important task?
2. Name one type of fire a firefighter must have knowledge of.
3. What is one sign of arson that a firefighter watches for?

Research Projects

1. Research the role of fire police. What is the complete list of this firefighter's responsibilities, and what special training does a member of the fire police receive?
2. Research the training required for firefighters in your community. How long is it, what does it involve, and what happens after firefighters complete the training?

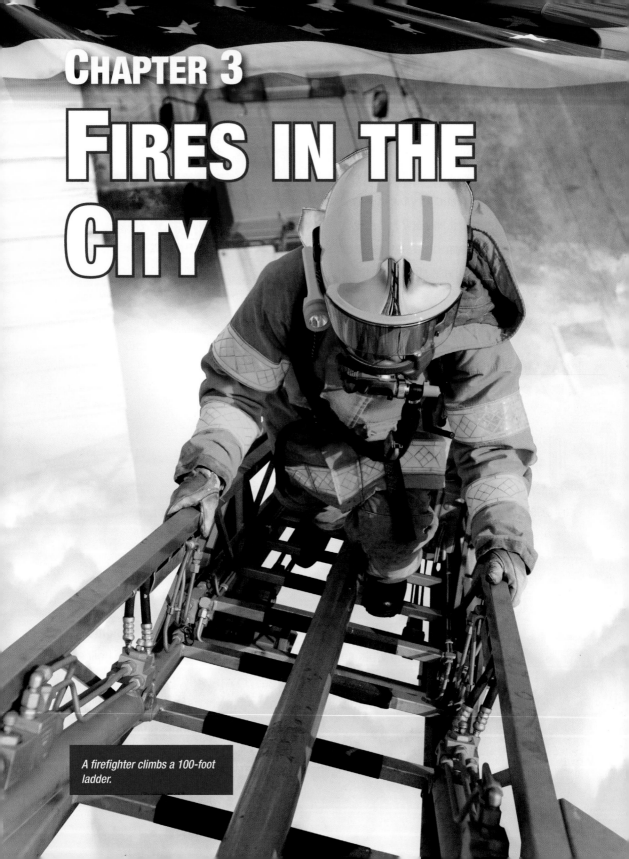

CHAPTER 3
FIRES IN THE CITY

A firefighter climbs a 100-foot ladder.

Today, millions of people live in cities, and that means hundreds of thousands of houses, apartment buildings, offices, schools, theaters, hospitals, hotels, department stores, and streets crowded with automobiles and buses. Fighting fires in cities presents a unique set of problems.

The first problem is getting fire engines to the scene of the fire as quickly as they can. This is why the engines sound loud alarms as they race through the streets and are allowed to drive through red traffic lights, while all other traffic has to stop. Engines do not have time to wait for the green light.

Getting to a Fire

Getting to a fire can mean driving several engines through the city streets. Two engines and one escape ladder may be all that is needed for a blaze in a single house, but larger buildings may require up to four engines and two ladders, or even more.

Fortunately, firefighters are good at finding their way around their own cities. They know where to find shortcuts through the back streets and how the streets join up with each other. They also know where to find the fire hydrants. The hydrant—a word that comes from the ancient Greek "hudor," meaning water—is a water pipe linked to a city's main water supply. Hydrants have nozzles to which firefighters can attach their hoses.

In the best scenario, firefighters can get hold of the plans, or already know the layout, of the building that is on fire. However, this is not always possible, especially in poorer city

Words to Understand

Extinguisher (fire): Metal container filled with chemicals used to put out a fire.

Inhabitants: Residents.

Multiple dwellings: Houses where more than one family lives.

Firefighters must access the closest fire hydrant to put a fire out quickly and efficiently.

districts. Even so, firefighters are familiar with the way fires behave and know in advance what they are likely to find when they reach the scene. Fire spreads upward, so a blaze on one floor of an apartment will soon spread to the apartment directly above it. Stairways are ready-made spaces for fire to climb up the inside of a building, so leaving the building that way is often impossible. Fire ladders placed against the outside walls must be used to enable the inhabitants to escape.

In addition, buildings are all too frequently constructed in ways that make it easy for fire to spread. For instance, the kitchen and bathroom are two rooms where there is a special danger of fire. In a big apartment building, these are often built one on top of the other. As a result, there are pipes that run up a building from the first floor to the top floor and, like stairways, these can help a fire reach upward through the building in a short time.

In Brooklyn, NY, where buildings are extremely close to one another, firefighters must establish a plan before they take action.

Multiple Dwellings and Private Dwellings

At the scene of a fire, a firefighter must first determine how many people are in danger. In cities, this usually means quite a large number. Buildings in which many people live are not necessarily skyscrapers; they are normally **multiple dwellings** no more than three or four stories high, housing three or more families. Firefighters have to assume that not everyone in the building will know it is on fire. So the first thing they do is search the floor where the fire has broken out and the floors above it. That way, they have a better chance of finding and rescuing the **inhabitants**, even if they have to wake them up in bed or get them out of the bathroom.

Ways to Fight the Fire

Ways to fight a fire can vary, depending on the equipment that is closest at hand. Suppose a television set, stove, or piece of furniture has burst into flames. People are advised to buy one or more **fire extinguishers** and place them in a prominent position in their rooms so they can grab them and use them as soon as a fire starts—but not everyone takes this advice. Even if there is a fire extinguisher in the building, it may be too far away. By the time someone retrieves it, the whole room, or the entire apartment or floor, could be on fire. The officer in charge of the firefighting team may not be able to stop this from happening, but he or she can order that a hose, which is much larger and more powerful than the average extinguisher, be brought up with all possible speed.

Most of the homes in which fires occur are not multiple dwellings. Fire is more likely to break out in **private dwellings**, where only one or two families live. They usually start on the first floor or in the basement, because this is where the equipment that causes most fires is likely to be found—stoves for cooking meals, the electricity supply, or the water heater. Another cause of fire is cigarettes. Many people smoke in their living rooms and bedrooms, and all it takes to start a fire is for a smoker to fall asleep and let a lighted cigarette drop on the carpet, furniture, or bedclothes.

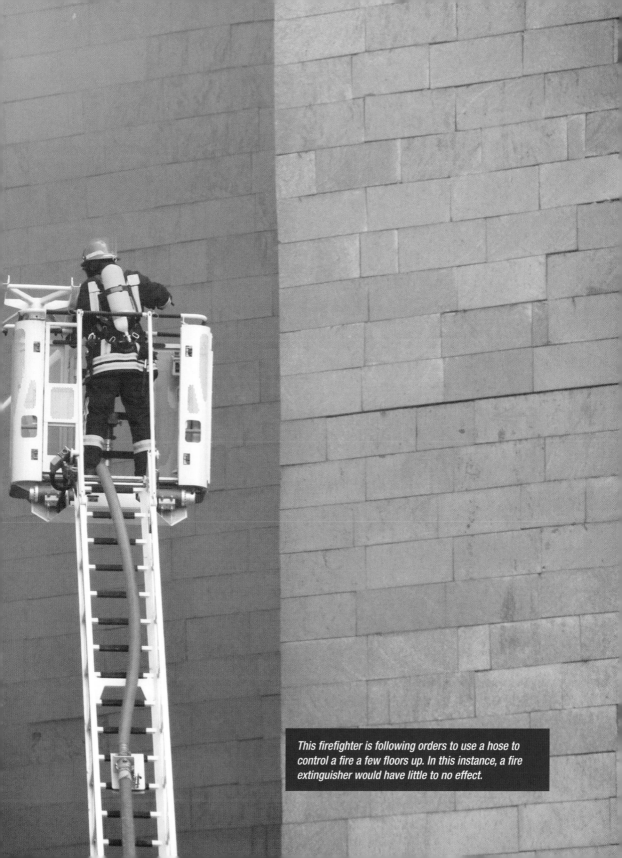

This firefighter is following orders to use a hose to control a fire a few floors up. In this instance, a fire extinguisher would have little to no effect.

Vent, Enter, Search

Finally, the firefighters perform what is called the VES routine. VES stands for "vent, enter, search." To vent a room, the windows are broken so that heat and smoke can escape. All shades, venetian blinds, and drapes, which could keep heat and smoke from getting out, are pulled away, and a ladder is placed at the side of the window to let the people inside climb down to safety.

"Enter" and "search" mean going into the rooms and searching them for any people who might be trapped inside. Sometimes, fire victims may be affected by the smoke and fumes, in which case, the firefighters will administer first aid. Once the VES routine is completed, the firefighters can concentrate on putting out the fire and making the building safe.

Fighting a fire in a high-rise building.

Firefighters breaking a window to vent a room engulfed in flames.

Witness to a City Fire

Around midnight in December, Jill Druse, daughter of a firefighter and wife of a newspaper reporter, went with her husband to the scene of a serious fire in Niles, MI. Even before they arrived, the fire had spread throughout the building, and the firefighters were in a great deal of danger. Jill watched them and later wrote of how much she admired them.

> I stood there and thought how selfless these men and women must be to risk their own lives in order to save someone else's [property]. I watched the men inside the building fight the smoke in order to dowse the fire. I also [realized] how much respect I have for all those men and women who strap on an air pack and go into a smoke-filled building never knowing if they will ever come out.

Inside A Burning Building

In his book, *Report from Engine Company 82*, Dennis Smith, a New York City firefighter in the South Bronx district, described how he fought a fire inside a burning building.

The fire was blazing away in three rooms at the end of the hall, and the smoke was so thick that Smith and another firefighter had to lie flat on the floor in order to find enough air to breathe. They managed to break down the door leading to one of the rooms and then directed their water hose inside to extinguish the flames. There was a loud sound of fire crackling, and as the water jet dislodged some plaster from the ceiling, pieces of it fell to the floor, hissing and steaming.

The fire, started deliberately by three young arsonists, was eventually put out, but two people died and another was badly injured. This was more than a fire: it was double homicide.

You can see from all this that there is much more to fighting fires than simply pouring on large amounts of water. Firefighters must first save lives. A fire may be put out, but firefighters have failed in their duty if, afterward, among the ashes, they find the bodies of victims they should have saved.

City Fires around the World

Each year, more fires break out in private dwellings than in big buildings. In 2013, 39.3 percent of the fires in the United States occurred outside, 31.7 percent occurred in private homes, and 14.5 percent were vehicle fires. At least 3,240 people were killed and another 15,925 were injured. Home fires tend to happen on weekends and between the hours of 6:00 p.m. and 7:00 p.m. December, January, and February were the worst months for fires because it was then, during the winter, that the heating was on in homes while people were asleep in bed.

The first sign of a fire is often the smoke it creates. However, despite a lot of advertising and advice from fire prevention authorities, in 2015, three of every five home fire deaths occurred in homes without smoke detectors. And where there is smoke, you will usually find a fire.

Buenos Aires, the capital of Argentina, is one of the most crowded cities on Earth—2.89 million inhabitants in 2016. The population of Mexico City, capital of Mexico, is almost as great—8.9 million inhabitants in 2016. Other big cities have smaller populations, but this still means a large number of people; for example, in 2016, there were 4 million living in Los Angeles and 2.87 million in Rome, Italy. Three of these cities (Mexico City, Tokyo, and Los Angeles) lie in earthquake zones. Serious earthquakes—measuring 6 or more on the Richter earthquake scale—not only wreck large areas of a city and kill people, they can also start fires.

An Oregon firefighter sprays a straight stream into a fully developed fire.

Text-Dependent Questions

1. Describe a fire hydrant and its function.
2. What is the first thing firefighters do when they arrive at an apartment fire?
3. What is one of the leading causes of house fires?

Research Projects

1. Hoverboards were a popular Christmas gift in December 2015. However, they became known as a fire hazard. Research why these gifts were prone to fires and how many fires actually occurred because of them.
2. The American Red Cross actively helps fire victims. Research what the organization's role is and how they help those who have been victims of a fire.

CHAPTER 4

WILDLAND FIRES

A plane provides air assistance in putting out a forest fire.

Nature can be very cruel. In the beautiful scenery of the wildlands, there lurk many possible dangers. Wildfires are just one, and they can inflict dreadful damage. For the reason that the wildlands are wild and unpopulated, there may be no one to notice a wildfire until it has taken hold over a large area.

The heat of summer can dry out the trees, leaves, and twigs, making it easier for a fire to break out. Careless visitors to the **wildlands** may easily start a fire, either by throwing a still-burning cigarette away on dry brushwood, or by failing to put out a campfire properly. Even a small piece of glass is dangerous; when the sun's rays shine on it, the glass concentrates the heat, and this can be enough to set alight brushwood, sticks, or vegetation.

A wildfire fighter recruitment video.

Dangerous Thunderstorms

Thunderstorms over the wildlands are particularly dangerous. A powerful bolt of lightning, with a temperature as high as 60,000°F (33,316°C), may strike just a single tree, bringing it crashing to the ground. As it falls, however, tiny flames may be burning inside it.

Words to Understand

Pall: Heavy fog or smoke causing the sky to be gloomy.

Wildfire: Fire in a wild area, such as a forest, that is not controlled and that can burn a large area quickly.

Wildlands: Land that is uncultivated or unfit for cultivation.

Lightning strikes can cause major damage.

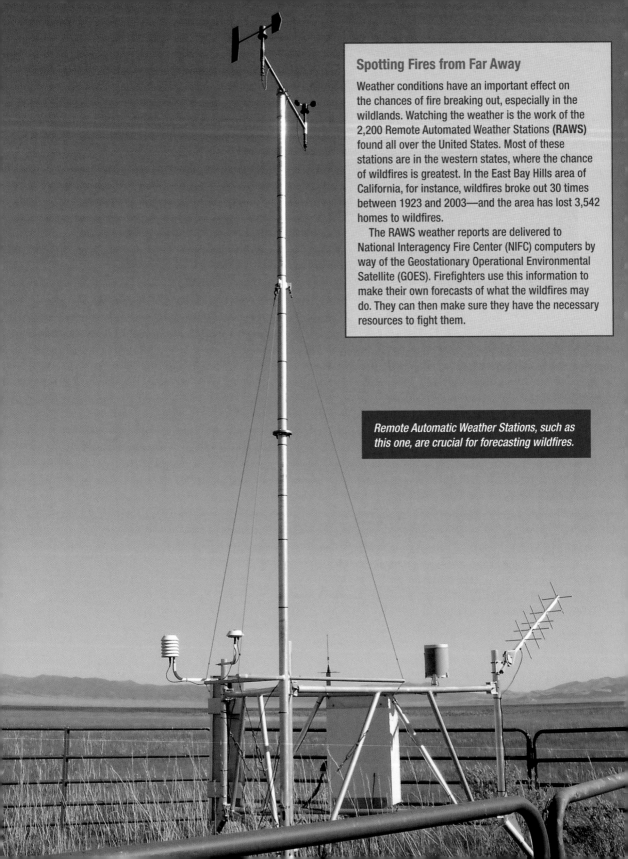

Spotting Fires from Far Away

Weather conditions have an important effect on the chances of fire breaking out, especially in the wildlands. Watching the weather is the work of the 2,200 Remote Automated Weather Stations **(RAWS)** found all over the United States. Most of these stations are in the western states, where the chance of wildfires is greatest. In the East Bay Hills area of California, for instance, wildfires broke out 30 times between 1923 and 2003—and the area has lost 3,542 homes to wildfires.

The RAWS weather reports are delivered to National Interagency Fire Center (NIFC) computers by way of the Geostationary Operational Environmental Satellite (GOES). Firefighters use this information to make their own forecasts of what the wildfires may do. They can then make sure they have the necessary resources to fight them.

Remote Automatic Weather Stations, such as this one, are crucial for forecasting wildfires.

The tiny flames from the falling tree can transfer themselves to dry vegetation. Before long, from this small beginning, an entire forest is ablaze.

Fortunately, weather forecasters can predict the arrival of thunderstorms over the wildlands. They can also identify those that have the greatest chance of starting a fire. In addition, the progress of lightning strikes can be tracked by computer; aircraft then fly over the area to check for smoke or flames.

Low- as well as high-tech methods can be used in detecting **wildfires**. In remote forests, tall fire towers have been built with observation platforms at the top. From these platforms, observers can see for miles around as they watch for signs of wildfire.

Sometimes, a fire can be left to burn itself out, but others are far too dangerous for that. Detecting big wildfires early is important, as is assessing the size of the blaze. Often, a serious wildfire is far too huge for local firefighting teams to handle, and others have to be called in from surrounding areas, sometimes from all over the country. Teams fighting wildfires can become utterly exhausted from the effort, not least because the fires so often seem to be one jump ahead of them. Fire can leap across roads and swamps and, if large enough, across lakes as well.

Wildfires also have an ally—the wind—which can direct the flames to fresh places, and so firefighters are faced with yet another blaze to handle. In addition, there is no supply of piped water in the wildlands, so water must be carried to the scene of the fire. Aircraft were first used in firefighting in California in 1919. If there is a lake near the fire scene, aircraft will scoop up water and transport it to the firefighters. Helicopters can hover over a lake while a hose is dropped into the water; this is a suction hose that sucks the water into a tank built into the underside of the helicopters. Helicopters also have their own water tanks or use big scoops, known as buckets, which can hold up to 400 gallons (1,514 L) of water.

Los Angeles firefighters work to stop wildfires from reaching their city.

Wildfire Damage

The months of May and June 1998 were unusually hot and dry in Florida. As a result, wildland fires broke out over many parts of the state. The situation was so serious that every one of the state's counties was declared a disaster area.

The damage was enormous. Around 26,000 acres (10,530 hectares) of farmland were burned. Farmers in northern Florida lost $80,000 worth of crops—corn, peanuts, cotton, watermelons, and soybeans. The heat of the fires ruined more crops, worth another $100 million. At least one person died, and some 30 people were injured, most of them from smoke inhalation or from burns.

Every day, around 80 new fires broke out, most of them caused by lightning. Some 500,000 acres (202,500 hectares) of forest were destroyed, and the smoke from the wildfire blotted out the sun as far away as Miami, 250 miles (402 km) distant. Fires reached towns and burned some 100 homes. Huge palls of smoke hung over Jacksonville, Daytona Beach, Tallahassee, and Orlando. In Jacksonville, 600 inhabitants were ordered to leave their homes, and another 150 in the town of Hampton were forced to do the same. Near the town of Waldo, the blaze stretched over a distance of 7 miles (11 km); fortunately, before it reached the town, the wind shifted and kept the flames away.

Although firefighters rushed to Florida from all over the United States, they were not able to put out the fires. All they could do was contain them; that is, make sure they spread no further before, eventually, they burned themselves out. There were 76 major wildfires (burning 10,000 acres or more) in Florida between 1998 and 2008.

A helicopter dips a large bucket into a body of water to fight a wildfire.

Helicopters and aircraft can also bring pumps or hoses and other equipment directly to the firefighters on the ground. In other aircraft, pilots fly over the wildfire and keep the ground crews informed about how quickly it is spreading and in what direction. In addition, the helicopters and aircraft can fight the fire themselves by dropping their cargo of water directly onto the flames. They may also drop "slurry," a fire retardant that slows the progress of a fire by reducing the supply of oxygen that lets the flames burn. Aircraft will often spray it all over a forest.

A firefighting aircraft drops water on a wildfire.

The Redmond Hotshots fight wildfires in Washington State.

The Hotshots

The people who fight wildland fires are often known as hotshots, and there may be hundreds of them tackling the blaze from the ground. They construct "fire lines" by taking away leaves or branches lying at the edge of the fire, then beating out the flames and spraying water on them: this helps keep the fire on the other side of the "line." The hotshots use radios to report

the progress of the fire, and aircraft follow its path, sometimes using thermal imaging cameras, which record the intensity of the heat in a variety of colors.

The temperatures the cameras record can be phenomenally high—as much as 2,000°F (1,093°C), and the hotshots have to be alert to many other dangers in a fire area. In hilly country, boulders can become dislodged and come tumbling down the hillsides toward them. Flaming branches, known as snags, may topple down from burning trees. If the smoke from the fire is extremely thick, the firefighters will have to crawl on their knees or lie flat on the ground, where there is some breathable air to be found.

Smokejumpers and Rappelers

When fires break out deep inside a forest, and as long as they are still relatively small, some firefighters, known as smokejumpers, parachute down into the area of the blaze. This is truly daredevil firefighting and it has to be done skillfully, or smokejumpers can be badly injured.

First of all, the aircraft pilot has to choose the area into which the smokejumpers are going to parachute. Then streamers are dropped so that the pilot can observe which way the winds are blowing. If they are blowing the fire toward the chosen target area, the smokejumpers cannot use it.

If the winds are favorable, the smokejumpers' heavy equipment is parachuted down, and the smokejumpers follow. Sometimes, they have to "thread the needle," which means going in to land among the trees. This is why smokejumpers wear special protective helmets with masks attached: they can be injured while coming down through the branches.

If the smokejumpers are falling too fast and need to slow down, they may have to do something really tricky—a "tree jump." The tree jump means coming down among the treetops so that the parachute gets caught in the branches. This, of course, stops the smokejumpers from crashing to the ground, but leaves them hanging high above it. They then use a rope to lower themselves to the ground.

Rappelers—the firefighters who carry out "rap attacks"—do not use parachutes. Instead, they use ropes suspended from a helicopter hovering up to 300 feet (90 m) from the ground. The special body harness they wear enables them to slide down the rope at a comfortable speed and, like the smokejumpers, they also wear protective helmets.

As they come in to land by rope, rappelers can seem a strange sight. They need hard hats to tackle fires, so they strap them to their legs and also carry bags containing equipment tied to their harnesses. Heavier equipment, like saws or pumps, can also be lowered down to the ground by a rope.

Valley rappelers in training.

Trapped by Fire

Sometimes, the firefighters themselves become trapped by a wildland fire. The blaze is all around them, the smoke chokes them, they feel they cannot breathe—but there is no obvious way out. Their only chance is to protect themselves from the flames or be consumed and die. In case this happens, firefighters attending wildland fires carry a fire shelter—a small tent made of aluminum foil and fiberglass specially made to keep away the flames, heat, and smoke. Once inside this tent, firefighters are able to survive, even when surrounded by the fire. They can wait until the blaze passes by, and then they can safely emerge.

Smokejumpers: elite firefighters.

Fighting a wildland fire is a long and exhausting business. Hotshots may have to work for up to 40 hours at a stretch. Even after a fire seems to be out, there is always the chance that a few tiny flames are still burning, ready to start yet another blaze. So the firefighters have to search around, sniffing the air for the smell of smoke and digging up small fires still burning underground and putting them out with water.

Text-Dependent Questions

1. What are RAWS and what do they do?
2. When and where were aircraft first used in firefighting?
3. Who are hotshots and what do they do?

Research Projects

1. Research the role of hotshots. How does a firefighter become a hotshot? Does it require special training?
2. Research the role of rappelers. How does a firefighter become a rappeler? Does it require special training?

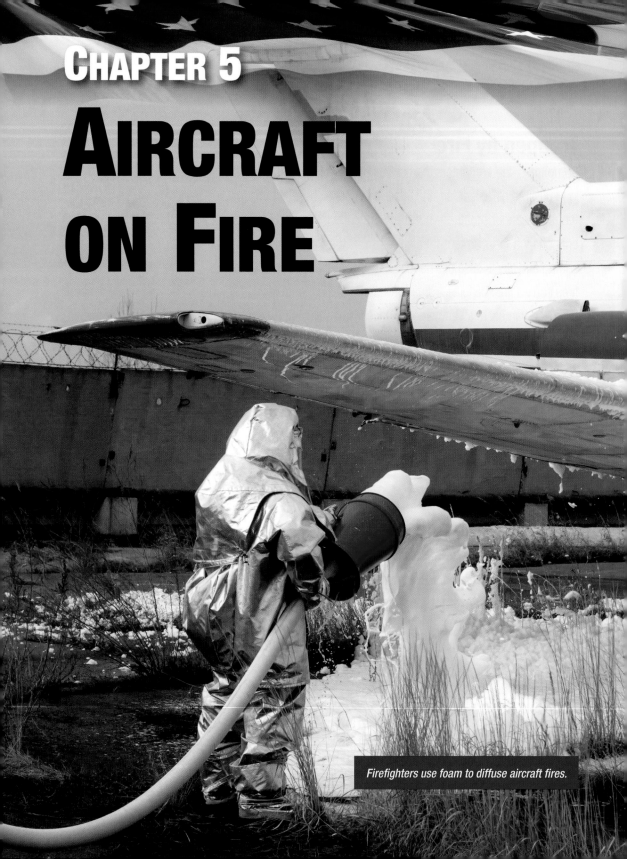

CHAPTER 5
AIRCRAFT ON FIRE

Firefighters use foam to diffuse aircraft fires.

Flying is often cited as the safest way to travel. One reason for this is that aircraft designers and manufacturers, as well as the airlines that carry millions of people around the world, have always been careful about safety. On board an aircraft, the passengers' seats are made of fireproof fabric, which burns less easily in a fire, or not at all. There are also smoke detectors, heat sensors, water sprinklers, and fire extinguishers for the crew to use.

If fire breaks out in places that cannot be reached—like the cargo hold or the fuel tanks, which are carried inside the wings—aircraft carry a supply of foam that can be used to flood these areas and put out the fire.

Before a flight takes off from an airport, passengers are shown how to put on life jackets in case the plane crashes into the sea. They also learn about using the oxygen masks the plane carries so that they will be able to breathe if the plane's outside "skin" is punctured, causing the pressure inside to drop.

When it comes to precautions against fire and other emergencies, the airlines try to anticipate what can go wrong and take steps in advance to prevent it. Unfortunately, accidents do happen, no matter how many precautions are taken. The fact that flying is considered the safest form of travel certainly means that the risk of fire or other accident has been reduced, but not that it has been completely eliminated.

Words to Understand

Aviation: Business or practice of flying airplanes.

Infrared: Producing or using rays that cannot be seen and that are longer than the rays producing red light.

Titanium: Very strong and light silvery metal.

Accidents Will Happen

Tragically, air crashes can cause multiple victims, but such a disaster is by no means inevitable. If an aircraft crashes at or near an airport, rescue and firefighting teams are already there to deal with it.

The teams at airports are usually small. This is not just because it is rare for aircraft to crash or make crash-landings on runways. Often, the traffic controllers at an airport know that an aircraft is in trouble because they are in contact with the pilot; so other teams can be alerted before the airplane tries to land.

Did You Know That . . .

When ships in harbor catch fire, fireboats are used to suck up water and throw it at the flames.
   Members of the crew on board ships are specially trained to deal with fires and hold regular fire drills.
   Railroad trains have special detectors fitted underneath the cars to look for signs of overheating that can start a fire.
   Along a railroad track, there are hotbox detectors that check all the cars passing along the rails for signs of overheating.
   When fire breaks out in an underground train, pipes called dry drops reach up to water hydrants in the street above.

Once alerted, the teams do not wait for the crash to occur. As soon as they learn of the emergency, they race across to the runway, monitoring the airplane's progress by radio. The teams use special vehicles to take them quickly to where the crash may take place. The most important are the foam pumpers, which carry pumps that can fight an aircraft fire using special foam. Foam is used because the aviation fuel used by aircraft causes hydrocarbon fires, which burn much more fiercely than the ordinary fuel in automobiles. Water alone cannot usually handle an aviation fuel fire.

A firefighting boat sprays jets of water onto a burning ship.

The Foam Pumpers

There are several of these foam-pumping vehicles. One is the rapid-intervention vehicle, which is quite fast and normally reaches the scene of the aircraft fire before the others. Larger foam pumpers can spray foam higher and farther—over a distance of about 75 yards (82 m)—using their tall turrets. There are also ground-sweep nozzles that spray foam all over the runway around the crashed airplane. This, as well as the foam and water that are sprayed over the fuselage to cool the aircraft down, makes it safer for passengers to escape through a special corridor that stretches down to the ground from the airplane's exit doors.

Putting out a jet plane fire.

Firefighters must be extremely cautious in approaching an aircraft fire because of the large quantities of jet fuel involved.

Concorde Crashes Near Paris

Air accidents can be caused by events no one can forecast. Such was the case when an Air France Concorde airliner crashed near Paris, France, after taking off for New York on July 25, 2000. All 109 passengers and crew and four people on the ground were killed.

Afterward, investigators discovered that a small piece of metal had fallen onto the runway from a Continental Airlines DC-10 "jumbo" jet that had taken off a few minutes previously. The metal ripped through one of the Concorde's tires, and debris from the tire hit one of the supersonic airliner's fuel tanks. The tank ruptured and the fuel ignited, setting the aircraft on fire.

Air France and British Airways, who also use Concordes, grounded their entire fleet. Before they were allowed to fly again, the Concordes were fitted with new extra-strength tires, and the insides of their fuel tanks were strengthened with a material called Kevlar, which is also used to make bulletproof vests.

After these improvements were made, the first Concorde to fly again took off from Paris for New York on November 8, 2001. The flight was successful and experienced no incidents, and there have been no incidents with Concordes as of 2016.

Some foam pumpers are so powerful that they can punch a hole in the aircraft's fuselage and pour their foam through it to put out any flames that are burning inside. If an aircraft has crashed at night, or if there is a lot of smoke swirling around, foam pumpers may also carry **infrared** cameras. These cameras enable the rescuers and firefighters to "see" through the dark and smoke.

Aircraft are often constructed from lightweight metals, such as titanium, which is, unfortunately, highly flammable. To combat this, the teams carry extinguishers specially made for extinguishing **titanium** fires. They may also pump dry chemicals over the aircraft to help put out the flames.

Fires in a crashed aircraft are not the only blazes firefighters have to worry about. The crash may have caused fuel to leak onto the ground, where it starts its own fire; foam and water have to be used to extinguish this fire before it can spread. Foam is particularly effective because it starves the fire of oxygen.

Saving Lives

As with all firefighting, the first thing to do is save lives—in this case, the lives of the passengers and crew. If the rescue teams have to enter the aircraft, they wait until the people stop coming out down the escape corridors. Of course, there may be injured passengers still inside the plane, but the teams have to be careful before going inside to search. If, for example, the aircraft's doors will not open, the teams may have to cut holes in the fuselage, and this will let air into the aircraft, which may cause fresh fires to start inside.

Disaster in New York City: Why Did the Twin Towers Collapse?

You only have to say the date—September 11, 2001—and everybody knows what you are talking about: the terrorist attacks on New York City and Washington, DC.

In New York City, the targets of the Al Qaeda terrorists and their leader, Osama bin Laden, were the soaring twin towers of the World Trade Center. Both towers eventually collapsed. The south tower went first, 45 minutes after the attack, and the north tower fell after 105 minutes. Within a matter of moments, nearly 3,000 people died. Only five people were found alive in the wreckage.

Why did the towers collapse? There are two main reasons. The first is that the tanks on board the aircraft were carrying a huge amount of aviation fuel—around 2,400 gallons (9,085 L) each—for long flights across the United States. This fuel ignited on impact with the towers, causing an enormous fire that reached temperatures of more than 2,700°F (1,482°C).

The second reason is the way in which the World Trade Center was built. Prior to 1966, which is when construction on the World Trade Center began, most skyscrapers, in New York and elsewhere in the world, had been built around a frame and were constructed of masonry, or stonework. The twin towers had no masonry and no frame. Instead, they had a tube structure, which meant that they were made of hollow steel columns: floor trusses, or struts, about 1.5 inches (4 cm) thick, extended from the outside of the towers to their center. This gave them much more floor space for offices than the masonry-built skyscrapers—as much as 40,000 square feet (4,860 sq m) extra per floor.

Tragically, however, this extra space helped the fire to spread rapidly and also incinerated people inside until there was nothing left of them. Once the floors and the struts beneath them melted in the intense heat, the tubular columns began to give way. Soon after, the floors collapsed, one on top of the other, until the whole building had crashed to the ground in a mess of rubble and debris.

The magnificent twin towers, the pride of the New York City skyline, had become the wasteland known as **Ground Zero.** Today this area of New York has become the National September 11 Memorial and Museum.

Firefighters and police inspect the aftermath of the Air France Concorde plane crash.

The inside of a crashed aircraft is a terrible mess, scattered with debris, luggage, and food carts. The rescuers and firefighters have to work their way through it all to make sure no one remains who is injured or who has been left behind. Even after the fires are out and the passengers and crew have gone, a crashed aircraft remains a danger. It may be soaked in **aviation** fuel, which can easily burst into flames while the wreckage is being removed for examination.

For this reason, the firefighters have to remain on standby for as long as investigators are at the scene. It is important for investigators to have a thorough look at the wreckage, because it provides clues about the cause of the crash. These clues can help prevent other aircraft from the same fate in the future.

Firefighters working near Ground Zero after the September 11 attacks on the World Trade Center.

Text-Dependent Questions

1. What is one of the safety procedures practiced by airlines?
2. What is a special vehicle used by firefighters at an airport?
3. What object do some vehicles carry that allow firefighters to see through smoke and at night?

Research Projects

1. Research firefighting teams at airports. How many firefighters are typically working? How often are they called to duty?
2. What is the average number of airplane or airport fires per year? What are the most common causes of these fires?

CHAPTER 6

FIREFIGHTING IN THE FUTURE

Fire hasn't changed, but technological advances provide better safer ways to control and extinguish

Today, technology progresses so fast that it often seems the future has already arrived. Modern firefighters now make use of an array of sophisticated equipment, and even the methods of firefighting are changing.

Firefighters wear new helmets made of light materials. They use cell phones, computers, satellites, and thermal imaging. Fire pumps now have gauges that do their own calculations to tell firefighters how fast they must pump water to put out the fire. A substance called Class A Foam is mixed with the water to extinguish fires faster than water alone and to keep the fire scene cooler for longer. The emergency medical services use the "doc in a box," a camera that can be plugged in inside a building where there is a fire victim. A doctor then looks at the picture on a TV screen and can recommend the appropriate treatment.

New firefighting methods are also being developed. For instance, instead of chopping a hole in a wall or door with a hatchet to see what is happening inside, firefighters will use instruments that can detect heat in a building. Sometimes, heat comes from people or animals; sometimes from a fire. The instruments will let the firefighters identify the heat source without having to make holes in walls, which may damage the building or put themselves or others at extra risk.

Words to Understand

Hotspot: Section of land with fire.

Interconnected: Joined or related.

Shape-shifting: Changes form at will.

> **Shape-Shifting Ice Robots**
>
> In the future, shape-shifting robots made of ice or of plates bolted to a frame will be used to fight fires. Firefighters will send the ice robots into a fire to melt over the blaze and reduce it or put it out.
>
> Other robots are made from several interconnected cubes, which lets them change their shape. These robots are enormously strong. If a ceiling in a burning building looks like it will collapse, they can be sent in to hold it up. As of 2016, robots are used primarily for search and rescue operations. Manned with cameras, they allow firefighters to see inside of potentially dangerous locations to see if there are people there that need to be rescued.

Wearing Sensors

Knowing how fast a fire is spreading is an important part of the firefighter's job. Up to now, they have mostly used their own experience to judge the rate of progress. This, no matter how experienced they are, can only be a matter of guesswork—but not anymore. Before long, firefighters will carry sensors on their visors or their clothing to tell them about heat and smoke levels, the direction of the wind, or the amount of poisonous fumes or harmful radiation produced by the fire. They may also carry small computers that will help them monitor the progress of a fire.

Advanced technology and new ways to use it will also be able to improve detection of those most extensive and difficult-to-handle fires—the wildfires that can spread so rapidly through forests and woods. Wildland fires are often considered to be the firefighter's greatest and most dangerous challenge. They flare up quietly, usually out of sight; start new fires even while the existing ones are being fought; create enormous damage; and, in some cases, threaten cities and towns, their homes, and inhabitants.

Sometimes, nature will come to the rescue and put out the flames with rain. This happened in 2001 when over 400 forest fires in northern Alberta, Canada, were under control, but not yet extinguished. The rain helped to put them out, but not before nearly 600 square miles (1,554 sq km) of land had been destroyed and hundreds of people had been forced to leave their homes.

A firefighting crew works a fire line to combat a wildfire near Los Angeles.

The Aerial Mobile Mapping System

Waiting for rain is not a satisfactory solution for firefighters, especially since it is often the absence of rainfall that helps wildland fires start in the first place. It is far better to use technology, which, unlike rainfall, can be controlled and directed at the fire. This is what Dr. Naser El-Sheimy of the University of Calgary, in Alberta, Canada, thought when he devised his Aerial Mobile Mapping System (AMMS). AMMS is not, in itself, new technology; it uses existing methods of firefighting and modern equipment and combines them with high-tech modern communications. Between them, these can detect remote, hidden "hotspots" in forests, which, if unnoticed and unattended, soon grow into big, serious fires.

AMMS works like this. The pilots of aircraft are provided with thermal (heat-seeking) cameras able to detect infrared radiation from a **hotspot**. As the aircraft flies over a forest, these cameras can pick up heat patterns, making it possible to find out exactly where the hotspots are. AMMS does need to be developed further. For instance, in June 2001, the system was still investigating how hotspots become big fires and how long it takes them to do so. As of 2016, the more prevalent technology used for aerial mapping uses drones, such as the ELIMCO E300. This drone is used in Spain to track wildfires at night.

City fires pose special challenges because buildings are close together and care must be taken to keep people in neighboring buildings safe.

City fires, of course, present an opposite problem from fires in the wildlands, where fire can work away unseen, destroying large uninhabited stretches of territory. The problem with city fires, as mentioned, is that there can be too many people around, thus increasing the danger of death or injury. In a shopping mall, for example, where a lot of people may be trapped inside, it can be difficult for firefighters to know what is going on. In the future, they will be able to use an infrared-color zoom lens fixed to a ladder to show them the scene.

Australia: Firefighting by Computer

In Australia, the New South Wales Fire Brigades (NSWFB) and the Science and Technology Laboratory of the Commonwealth Scientific and Industrial Research Organization (CSIRO) have undertaken a lot of computerized research. They have built up a big database, known as AIRS—the Australian Incident Reporting System—using information from a million or more fires that have occurred since 1990. This provides a wide-ranging picture of how fires spread, how hazardous materials behave in fire situations, how to rescue fire victims, and every other detail involved in fire emergencies. All this information can be accessed as a guide to fighting future fires.

The database also provides the chance for further research. For instance, firefighters may report on the thickness or the height of walls or the strength of a fire door in a house. This information can then be used to examine the structure of buildings, which may lead to new designs that provide better protection.

Even fire training will benefit from future technology. Teachers will not need to have a real burning building to help trainees learn how to fight fires: they will be able to use virtual reality instead. Although not the real thing, this will be an invaluable training aid.

In the future, too, houses can carry their own fire detection systems. These are different from smoke detectors, which give warning of a fire, but do not say exactly where it is. The new detectors can be placed in the rooms of a house, and if a fire breaks out, they will tell firefighters exactly where it is.

Fire Spy, The Robot Firefighter

Firefighters face enormous dangers when they go to the scene of a fire: collapsing ceilings, fumes from poisonous chemicals, or the risk of getting trapped by the blaze they are trying to control. In the future, however, machines are going to take over in the shape of Fire Spy, the Robot Firefighter. Fire Spy can be controlled from a safe distance, more than 300 feet (91 m) away, and enters a building on fire to search for chemicals or other materials that are flammable. Fire Spy will provide a safe way of removing these materials to places well away from the fire without firefighters having to risk their lives to do it.

The West Yorkshire Fire Service in Britain learned about the tremendous risks involved when they fought a fire at a chemical factory in the city of Bradford in 1992. One of the factory's warehouses contained 600 tons (540 metric tonnes) of the chemical acrylo-nitryl. Acrylo-nitryl is a powerful explosive, and the Fire Service believes that if it had blown up, large areas of the city of Bradford would have been destroyed.

Fortunately, the acrylo-nitryl did not explode, but another fire could bring the same danger. This is where Fire Spy will help. Fire Spy was designed to work in temperatures that human beings cannot survive—up to 1,500°F (816°C). The robot has a strong, grabbing arm in front and is equipped with infrared and ordinary cameras, which can send back pictures to a video screen. In this way, the firefighter controlling Fire Spy can see what is happening inside the burning building and where the flammable materials are.

In 2016, several forms of firefighting robots were under development or various phases of use. One includes the Fire Ox, designed and manufactured by Lockheed Martin. It has an onboard water tank and is designed for use in wildfires and hazardous material fires.

From Bucket Brigades to Beyond

It is not practical, of course, to think that all fires can be prevented, however much modern technology is used in the fight against them. Fire has always been a wild spirit with a will of its own and a terrifying ability to destroy and devastate wherever it goes. Indeed, in ancient times, fire was regarded as a god, for it had such a terrible, all-consuming power over human life.

Firefighting has come a long way since then, especially in the recent past. After all, only three centuries have passed since fires were being fought by the age-old method of bucket brigades—and not always successfully, either. Technology has produced better pumps or better water supplies, and these have played their part in improving firefighting methods, but it is high tech that has made the biggest difference. For the first time in history, it has given firefighters and fire victims a real chance to get the better of fire. As this technology progresses, those chances are going to increase in the 21st century and beyond.

Mask gives firefighters "bionic" vision.

Text-Dependent Questions

1. Name one way robots are being used to fight fires.
2. What is AMMS and how does it function?
3. What is the Fire Ox?

Research Projects

1. Select one of the new technologies discussed in this chapter and gather more information about it. If it isn't currently being used to fight fires, when will it be? How expensive will it be to purchase?
2. How are computers used in firefighting today? What goals do they achieve? Are there plans to expand their use?

Series Glosssary

Air marshal: Armed guard traveling on an aircraft to protect the passengers and crew; the air marshal is often disguised as a passenger.

Annexation: To incorporate a country or other territory within the domain of a state.

Armory: A supply of arms for defense or attack.

Assassinate: To murder by sudden or secret attack, usually for impersonal reasons.

Ballistic: Of or relating to firearms.

Biological warfare: Also known as germ warfare, this is war fought with biotoxins—harmful bacteria or viruses that are artificially propagated and deliberately dispersed to spread sickness among an enemy.

Cartel: A combination of groups with a common action or goal.

Chemical warfare: The use of poisonous or corrosive substances to kill or incapacitate the enemy; it differs from biological warfare in that the chemicals concerned are not organic, living germs.

Cold War: A long and bitter enmity between the United States and the Free World and the Soviet Union and its Communist satellites, which went on from 1945 to the collapse of Communism in 1989.

Communism: A system of government in which a single authoritarian party controls state-owned means of production.

Conscription: Compulsory enrollment of persons especially for military service.

Consignment: A shipment of goods or weapons.

Contingency operations: Operations of a short duration and most often performed at short notice, such as dropping supplies into a combat zone.

Counterintelligence: Activities designed to collect information about enemy espionage and then to thwart it.

Covert operations: Secret plans and activities carried out by spies and their agencies.

Cyberterrorism: A form of terrorism that seeks to cause disruption by interfering with computer networks.

Democracy: A government elected to rule by the majority of a country's people.

Depleted uranium: One of the hardest known substances, it has most of its radioactivity removed before being used to make bullets.

Dissident: A person who disagrees with an established religious or political system, organization, or belief.

Embargo: A legal prohibition on commerce.

Emigration: To leave one country to move to another country.

Extortion: The act of obtaining money or other property from a person by means of force or intimidation.

Extradite: To surrender an alleged criminal from one state or nation to another having jurisdiction to try the charge.

Federalize/federalization: The process by which National Guard units, under state command in normal circumstances, are called up by the president in times of crisis to serve the federal government of the United States as a whole.

Genocide: The deliberate and systematic destruction of a racial, political, or cultural group.

Guerrilla: A person who engages in irregular warfare, especially as a member of an independent unit carrying out harassment and sabotage.

Hijack: To take unlawful control of a ship, train, aircraft, or other form of transport.

Immigration: The movement of a person or people ("immigrants") into a country; as opposed to emigration, their movement out.

Indict: To charge with a crime by the finding or presentment of a jury (as a grand jury) in due form of law.

Infiltrate: To penetrate an organization, like a terrorist network.

Infrastructure: The crucial networks of a nation, such as transportation and communication, and also including government organizations, factories, and schools.

Insertion: Getting into a place where hostages are being held.

Insurgent: A person who revolts against civil authority or an established government.

Internment: To hold someone, especially an immigrant, while his or her application for residence is being processed.

Logistics: The aspect of military science dealing with the procurement, maintenance, and transportation of military matériel, facilities, and personnel.

Matériel: Equipment, apparatus, and supplies used by an organization or institution.

Militant: Having a combative or aggressive attitude.

Militia: a military force raised from civilians, which supports a regular army in times of war.

Narcoterrorism: Outrages arranged by drug trafficking gangs to destabilize government, thus weakening law enforcement and creating conditions for the conduct of their illegal business.

NATO: North Atlantic Treaty Organization; an organization of North American and European countries formed in 1949 to protect one another against possible Soviet aggression.

Naturalization: The process by which a foreigner is officially "naturalized," or accepted as a U.S. citizen.

Nonstate actor: A terrorist who does not have official government support.

Ordnance: Military supplies, including weapons, ammunition, combat vehicles, and maintenance tools and equipment.

Refugee: A person forced to take refuge in a country not his or her own, displaced by war or political instability at home.

Rogue state: A country, such as Iraq or North Korea, that ignores the conventions and laws set by the international community; rogue states often pose a threat, either through direct military action or by harboring terrorists.

Sortie: One mission or attack by a single plane.

Sting: A plan implemented by undercover police in order to trap criminals.

Surveillance: To closely watch over and monitor situations; the USAF employs many different kinds of surveillance equipment and techniques in its role as an intelligence gatherer.

Truce: A suspension of fighting by agreement of opposing forces.

UN: United Nations; an international organization, of which the United States is a member, that was established in 1945 to promote international peace and security.

Chronology

ca. 4000 BCE: The establishment of the first cities in Mesopotamia (Iraq) increases the risk of fire because so many people now live close together.

2nd century: Leather water pumps for firefighting are used in ancient Egypt.

CE 61: Rebel queen Boudicca of the Iceni burns London, in the Roman province of Britannia.

CE 63: Roman vigiles in London watch out for fires.

CE 64: Great fire in ancient Rome; Emperor Nero is blamed for starting it.

CE 390: Fire at Alexandria, Egypt, destroys the 700,000 books of the city library.

CE 872: King Alfred of Wessex (southern England) introduces the curfew. *Curfew* comes from the French *couvre-feu*, cover fire. People now had to put covers over their household fires at night to protect against the risk of fire.

1212: London Bridge burns down.

1648: Fire inspectors are appointed in New Amsterdam (New York) to make sure fire regulations are observed.

1650: First fire engine—a tub filled with water and having a pump for pouring water on fires.

1666: Great Fire of London, which destroyed most of the city.

1680: First fire brigade is established in London; first fire brigade established in Boston, MA.

1735: Benjamin Franklin organizes the first volunteer fire brigade in America.

1765: Future president George Washington brings the first fire engine to America from Britain.

1818: Molly Williams becomes the first woman firefighter in the United States.

1820: In York (now Toronto, Canada), every householder is ordered to keep two buckets for carrying water to fires.

1829: First steam-driven fire engine.

1870: Ladders are first used to fight fire in the higher stories of buildings.

1871: Great Chicago Fire.

1906: San Francisco earthquake and fire.

ca. 1918: First firefighting departments.

1919: Aircraft first used to fight fires in California.

1991: Two serious wildland fires in East Bay Hills area, CA.

1994: Forest fire on Storm King Mountain, CO.

1994: Earthquake and fires in Los Angeles.

1998: Huge wildland fires in northern Florida and New Mexico.

2000: July 25, crash of Air France Concorde, Paris.

2000–2001: Serious fires in the forests of Alberta, Canada.

2001: September 11, the twin towers of the World Trade Center, New York City, collapse after two airplanes fly directly into them.

2006: Fire in Los Angeles and Ventura Counties, CA.

2012: Six-alarm fire created by Hurricane Sandy destroys more than 100 homes in New Jersey.

2013: Arson is the cause of the West Fertilizer plant fire in West, TX.

Further Resources

Websites

Fire disasters: forestry/about.com/library/weekly/aa052100.htm

Firefighting robots: easyweb.easynet.co.uk

Fire on the Mountain (South Canyon Fire, 1994): www.wildfire news.com/fireonthemountain/

Fire research: www.dbce.csiro.au/inno-web/0800/fire_research.htm

Florida Fires (2001): www.canoe.ca/CNEWSScienceNews/fire_ may29-cp.html

International Association of Firefighters: client.prod.iaff.org/

Further Reading

Dickman, Kyle. *On the Burning Edge: A Fateful Fire and the Men Who Fought It.* New York: Ballantine Books, 2015.

Egan, Timothy. *The Big Burn: Teddy Roosevelt and the Fire That Saved America.* New York: Mariner Books, 2010.

Gorell, Gena K. *Catching Fire: The Story of Firefighting.* Toronto, ON: Tundra Books, 1999.

Norman, John. *Fire Officer's Handbook of Tactics.* NJ: Fire Engineering Books, Pennwell Books, 1998.

Paul, Caroline. *Fighting Fire.* New York: St. Martin's Press, 1999.

Pickett, George. *The Brave: A Story of New York City's Firefighters.* Fredericksburg, VA: Brick Tower Press, 2002.

Smith, D. *Firefighters: Their Lives in Their Own Words.* New York: Broadway Books, 2002.

Taylor, Murry A. *Jumping Fire: A Smokejumper's Memoir of Fighting Wildfire.* Philadelphia: Harvest Books, 2001.

Index

About the Author

Brenda Ralph Lewis is a prolific writer of books, articles, television documentary scripts, and other materials on history, royalty, military subjects, aviation, and philately. Her writing includes many books on ancient history, culture, and life; books on World War II: *The Hitler Youth: The* Hitlerjugend *in Peace and War 1933–1945* (2000), *Women At War* (2001), and *The Story of Anne Frank* (2001). She has also written or contributed to numerous books for children, including *The Aztecs* (1999), *Stamps! A Young Philatelist's Guide* (1998), and *Ritual Sacrifice: A History* (2002). She lives in Buckinghamshire, England.

About the Consultant

Manny Gomez, an expert on terrorism and security, is President of MG Security Services and a former Principal Relief Supervisor and Special Agent with the FBI. He investigated terrorism and espionage cases as an agent in the National Security Division. He was a certified undercover agent and successfully completed Agent Survival School. Chairman of the Board of the National Law Enforcement Association (NLEA), Manny is also a former Sergeant in the New York Police Department (NYPD) where he supervised patrol and investigative activities of numerous police officers, detectives and civilian personnel. Mr. Gomez worked as a uniformed and plainclothes officer in combating narcotics trafficking, violent crimes, and quality of life concerns. He has executed over 100 arrests and received Departmental recognition on eight separate occasions. Mr. Gomez has a Bachelor's Degree and Master's Degree and is a graduate of Fordham University School of Law where he was on the Dean's list. He is admitted to the New York and New Jersey Bar. He served honorably in the United States Marine Corps infantry.